# THE ADVENTURE STARTS HERE!

## Travel Journal and Planner

**Activinotes**

***Activinotes***

DAILY JOURNALS, PLANNERS, NOTEBOOKS AND OTHER BLANK BOOKS

# Travel Adventure Starts Here!

## pre-travel checklist

## packing checklist

venue
travel date/time

travel buddy
transportation

hotel reservation
contact person/number

travel cost
travel budget

Things to See & Do :

☐ . . . . . . . . . . . . . . . . . . . . . . . . . . .     ☐ . . . . . . . . . . . . . . . . . . . . . . . . . . .
☐ . . . . . . . . . . . . . . . . . . . . . . . . . . .     ☐ . . . . . . . . . . . . . . . . . . . . . . . . . . .
☐ . . . . . . . . . . . . . . . . . . . . . . . . . . .     ☐ . . . . . . . . . . . . . . . . . . . . . . . . . . .
☐ . . . . . . . . . . . . . . . . . . . . . . . . . . .     ☐ . . . . . . . . . . . . . . . . . . . . . . . . . . .
☐ . . . . . . . . . . . . . . . . . . . . . . . . . . .     ☐ . . . . . . . . . . . . . . . . . . . . . . . . . . .

Adventures to Have :

☐ . . . . . . . . . . . . . . . . . . .
☐ . . . . . . . . . . . . . . . . . . .
☐ . . . . . . . . . . . . . . . . . . .
☐ . . . . . . . . . . . . . . . . . . .
☐ . . . . . . . . . . . . . . . . . . .
☐ . . . . . . . . . . . . . . . . . . .
☐ . . . . . . . . . . . . . . . . . . .

Things to Observe :

☐ . . . . . . . . . . . . . . . . . . . . . . .
☐ . . . . . . . . . . . . . . . . . . . . . . .
☐ . . . . . . . . . . . . . . . . . . . . . . .
☐ . . . . . . . . . . . . . . . . . . . . . . .
☐ . . . . . . . . . . . . . . . . . . . . . . .
☐ . . . . . . . . . . . . . . . . . . . . . . .
☐ . . . . . . . . . . . . . . . . . . . . . . .
☐ . . . . . . . . . . . . . . . . . . . . . . .

Places to Mingle :

☐ . . . . . . . . . . . . . . . . . . .
☐ . . . . . . . . . . . . . . . . . . .
☐ . . . . . . . . . . . . . . . . . . .
☐ . . . . . . . . . . . . . . . . . . .
☐ . . . . . . . . . . . . . . . . . . .
☐ . . . . . . . . . . . . . . . . . . .
☐ . . . . . . . . . . . . . . . . . . .

Shops to Visit :

☐ . . . . . . . . . . . . . . . . . .
☐ . . . . . . . . . . . . . . . . . .
☐ . . . . . . . . . . . . . . . . . .
☐ . . . . . . . . . . . . . . . . . .
☐ . . . . . . . . . . . . . . . . . .
☐ . . . . . . . . . . . . . . . . . .
☐ . . . . . . . . . . . . . . . . . .

Streets to Check Out :

☐ . . . . . . . . . . . . . . . . . . . .     ☐ . . . . . . . . . . . . . . . . . .
☐ . . . . . . . . . . . . . . . . . . . .     ☐ . . . . . . . . . . . . . . . . . .
☐ . . . . . . . . . . . . . . . . . . . .     ☐ . . . . . . . . . . . . . . . . . .

| Date | Itinerary | Reservation |
|------|-----------|-------------|
|      |           |             |
|      |           |             |
|      |           |             |
|      |           |             |
|      |           |             |
|      |           |             |
|      |           |             |
|      |           |             |
|      |           |             |
|      |           |             |
|      |           |             |
|      |           |             |
|      |           |             |
|      |           |             |

## Notes

# Journal

# Travel Adventure Starts Here!

## pre-travel checklist

## packing checklist

Contacts

---

venue
travel date/time

_____

travel buddy
transportation

_____

hotel reservation
contact person/number

_____

travel cost
travel budget

_____

Things to See & Do :

☐..............................   ☐..............................
☐..............................   ☐..............................
☐..............................   ☐..............................
☐..............................   ☐..............................
☐..............................   ☐..............................

Adventures to Have :

☐.......................
☐.......................
☐.......................   Things to Observe :
☐.......................
☐.......................   ☐..............................
☐.......................   ☐..............................
☐.......................   ☐..............................
                          ☐..............................
                          ☐..............................
                          ☐..............................
                          ☐..............................

Places to Mingle :

☐.......................
☐.......................
☐.......................
☐.......................                    Shops to Visit :
☐.......................
☐.......................   ☐.......................
☐.......................   ☐.......................
                          ☐.......................
Streets to Check Out :    ☐.......................
                          ☐.......................
                          ☐.......................
                          ☐.......................

☐.......................   ☐.......................
☐.......................   ☐.......................
☐.......................   ☐.......................

| Date | Itinerary | Reservation |
|------|-----------|-------------|
|      |           |             |
|      |           |             |
|      |           |             |
|      |           |             |
|      |           |             |
|      |           |             |
|      |           |             |
|      |           |             |
|      |           |             |
|      |           |             |
|      |           |             |
|      |           |             |
|      |           |             |

**Notes**

# Journal

# Travel Adventure Starts Here!

## pre-travel checklist

## packing checklist

Contacts

venue
travel date/time

travel buddy
transportation

hotel reservation
contact person/number

travel cost
travel budget

Things to See & Do :

☐ ...................................
☐ ...................................
☐ ...................................
☐ ...................................
☐ ...................................

☐ ...................................
☐ ...................................
☐ ...................................
☐ ...................................
☐ ...................................

Adventures to Have :

☐ ...........................
☐ ...........................
☐ ...........................
☐ ...........................
☐ ...........................
☐ ...........................
☐ ...........................

Things to Observe :

☐ ...................................
☐ ...................................
☐ ...................................
☐ ...................................
☐ ...................................
☐ ...................................
☐ ...................................
☐ ...................................

Places to Mingle :

☐ ...........................
☐ ...........................
☐ ...........................
☐ ...........................
☐ ...........................
☐ ...........................
☐ ...........................

Shops to Visit :

☐ ...........................
☐ ...........................
☐ ...........................
☐ ...........................
☐ ...........................
☐ ...........................
☐ ...........................

Streets to Check Out :

☐ .......................
☐ .......................
☐ .......................

☐ .......................
☐ .......................
☐ .......................

| Date | Itinerary | Reservation |
|------|-----------|-------------|
|      |           |             |
|      |           |             |
|      |           |             |
|      |           |             |
|      |           |             |
|      |           |             |
|      |           |             |
|      |           |             |
|      |           |             |
|      |           |             |
|      |           |             |
|      |           |             |
|      |           |             |

## Notes

# Journal

# Travel Adventure Starts Here!

## pre-travel checklist

## packing checklist

venue
travel date/time

travel buddy
transportation

hotel reservation
contact person/number

travel cost
travel budget

Things to See & Do :

☐ ...................................
☐ ...................................
☐ ...................................
☐ ...................................
☐ ...................................

☐ ...................................
☐ ...................................
☐ ...................................
☐ ...................................
☐ ...................................

Adventures to Have :

☐ ...............................
☐ ...............................
☐ ...............................
☐ ...............................
☐ ...............................
☐ ...............................
☐ ...............................

Things to Observe :

☐ ...................................
☐ ...................................
☐ ...................................
☐ ...................................
☐ ...................................
☐ ...................................
☐ ...................................

Places to Mingle :

☐ ...............................
☐ ...............................
☐ ...............................
☐ ...............................
☐ ...............................
☐ ...............................
☐ ...............................

Shops to Visit :

☐ ...........................
☐ ...........................
☐ ...........................
☐ ...........................
☐ ...........................
☐ ...........................
☐ ...........................

Streets to Check Out :

☐ ......................
☐ ......................
☐ ......................

☐ ....................
☐ ....................
☐ ....................

| Date | Itinerary | Reservation |
|---|---|---|
| | | |
| | | |
| | | |
| | | |
| | | |
| | | |
| | | |
| | | |
| | | |
| | | |
| | | |
| | | |
| | | |

## Notes

# Journal

# Travel Adventure Starts Here!

## pre-travel checklist

## packing checklist

venue
travel date/time

travel buddy
transportation

hotel reservation
contact person/number

travel cost
travel budget

Things to See & Do :

- ............................................
- ............................................
- ............................................
- ............................................
- ............................................

- ............................................
- ............................................
- ............................................
- ............................................
- ............................................

Adventures to Have :

- ............................................
- ............................................
- ............................................
- ............................................
- ............................................
- ............................................
- ............................................

Things to Observe :

- ............................................
- ............................................
- ............................................
- ............................................
- ............................................
- ............................................
- ............................................
- ............................................

Places to Mingle :

- ............................................
- ............................................
- ............................................
- ............................................
- ............................................
- ............................................
- ............................................

Shops to Visit :

- ............................................
- ............................................
- ............................................
- ............................................
- ............................................
- ............................................

Streets to Check Out :

- ............................................
- ............................................
- ............................................

- ............................................
- ............................................
- ............................................

| Date | Itinerary | Reservation |
|---|---|---|
| | | |
| | | |
| | | |
| | | |
| | | |
| | | |
| | | |
| | | |
| | | |
| | | |
| | | |
| | | |
| | | |

## Notes

# Journal

# Travel Adventure Starts Here!

## pre-travel checklist

## packing checklist

Contacts

---

venue
travel date/time

_____

travel buddy
transportation

_____

hotel reservation
contact person/number

_____

travel cost
travel budget

_____

Things to See & Do :

☐.............................  ☐.............................
☐.............................  ☐.............................
☐.............................  ☐.............................
☐.............................  ☐.............................
☐.............................  ☐.............................

Adventures to Have :

☐.........................
☐.........................
☐.........................
☐.........................
☐.........................
☐.........................
☐.........................

Things to Observe :

☐.............................
☐.............................
☐.............................
☐.............................
☐.............................
☐.............................
☐.............................
☐.............................

Places to Mingle :

☐.........................
☐.........................
☐.........................
☐.........................
☐.........................
☐.........................
☐.........................

Shops to Visit :

☐.....................
☐.....................
☐.....................
☐.....................
☐.....................
☐.....................
☐.....................

Streets to Check Out :

☐......................  ☐....................
☐......................  ☐....................
☐......................  ☐....................

| Date | Itinerary | Reservation |
|------|-----------|-------------|
|      |           |             |
|      |           |             |
|      |           |             |
|      |           |             |
|      |           |             |
|      |           |             |
|      |           |             |
|      |           |             |
|      |           |             |
|      |           |             |
|      |           |             |
|      |           |             |
|      |           |             |

## Notes

# Journal

# Travel Adventure Starts Here!

## pre-travel checklist

## packing checklist

venue
travel date/time

travel buddy
transportation

hotel reservation
contact person/number

travel cost
travel budget

Things to See & Do :

☐ ................................
☐ ................................
☐ ................................
☐ ................................
☐ ................................

☐ ................................
☐ ................................
☐ ................................
☐ ................................
☐ ................................

Adventures to Have :

☐ ............................
☐ ............................
☐ ............................
☐ ............................
☐ ............................
☐ ............................
☐ ............................

Things to Observe :

☐ ................................
☐ ................................
☐ ................................
☐ ................................
☐ ................................
☐ ................................
☐ ................................

Places to Mingle :

☐ ............................
☐ ............................
☐ ............................
☐ ............................
☐ ............................
☐ ............................
☐ ............................

Shops to Visit :

☐ ..........................
☐ ..........................
☐ ..........................
☐ ..........................
☐ ..........................
☐ ..........................
☐ ..........................

Streets to Check Out :

☐ ........................
☐ ........................
☐ ........................

☐ ........................
☐ ........................
☐ ........................

| Date | Itinerary | Reservation |
|------|-----------|-------------|
|      |           |             |
|      |           |             |
|      |           |             |
|      |           |             |
|      |           |             |
|      |           |             |
|      |           |             |
|      |           |             |
|      |           |             |
|      |           |             |
|      |           |             |
|      |           |             |
|      |           |             |

## Notes

Journal

# Travel Adventure Starts Here!

## pre-travel checklist

## packing checklist

venue
travel date/time

travel buddy
transportation

hotel reservation
contact person/number

travel cost
travel budget

Things to See & Do :

☐ ...................................  ☐ ...................................
☐ ...................................  ☐ ...................................
☐ ...................................  ☐ ...................................
☐ ...................................  ☐ ...................................
☐ ...................................  ☐ ...................................

Adventures to Have :

☐ ...............................
☐ ...............................
☐ ...............................
☐ ...............................
☐ ...............................
☐ ...............................
☐ ...............................

Things to Observe :

☐ ...................................
☐ ...................................
☐ ...................................
☐ ...................................
☐ ...................................
☐ ...................................
☐ ...................................

Places to Mingle :

☐ ...............................
☐ ...............................
☐ ...............................
☐ ...............................
☐ ...............................
☐ ...............................
☐ ...............................

Shops to Visit :

☐ ...........................
☐ ...........................
☐ ...........................
☐ ...........................
☐ ...........................
☐ ...........................
☐ ...........................

Streets to Check Out :

☐ ...........................  ☐ .......................
☐ ...........................  ☐ .......................
☐ ...........................  ☐ .......................

| Date | Itinerary | Reservation |
|------|-----------|-------------|
|      |           |             |
|      |           |             |
|      |           |             |
|      |           |             |
|      |           |             |
|      |           |             |
|      |           |             |
|      |           |             |
|      |           |             |
|      |           |             |
|      |           |             |
|      |           |             |
|      |           |             |

## Notes

# Journal

# Travel Adventure Starts Here!

## pre-travel checklist

## packing checklist

Contacts

venue
travel date/time

_____

travel buddy
transportation

_____

hotel reservation
contact person/number

_____

travel cost
travel budget

_____

Things to See & Do :

☐ ........................... ☐ ...........................
☐ ........................... ☐ ...........................
☐ ........................... ☐ ...........................
☐ ........................... ☐ ...........................
☐ ........................... ☐ ...........................

Adventures to Have :

☐ .........................
☐ .........................
☐ .........................
☐ .........................
☐ .........................
☐ .........................
☐ .........................

Things to Observe :

☐ ...........................
☐ ...........................
☐ ...........................
☐ ...........................
☐ ...........................
☐ ...........................
☐ ...........................

Places to Mingle :

☐ .........................
☐ .........................
☐ .........................
☐ .........................
☐ .........................
☐ .........................
☐ .........................

Shops to Visit :

☐ .........................
☐ .........................
☐ .........................
☐ .........................
☐ .........................
☐ .........................
☐ .........................

Streets to Check Out :

☐ ....................... ☐ .......................
☐ ....................... ☐ .......................
☐ ....................... ☐ .......................

| Date | Itinerary | Reservation |
| --- | --- | --- |
| | | |
| | | |
| | | |
| | | |
| | | |
| | | |
| | | |
| | | |
| | | |
| | | |
| | | |
| | | |
| | | |

## Notes

# Journal

# Travel Adventure Starts Here!

## pre-travel checklist

## packing checklist

Contacts

---

venue
travel date/time

_____

travel buddy
transportation

_____

hotel reservation
contact person/number

_____

travel cost
travel budget

_____

Things to See & Do :

- ☐ .............................
- ☐ .............................
- ☐ .............................
- ☐ .............................
- ☐ .............................

- ☐ .............................
- ☐ .............................
- ☐ .............................
- ☐ .............................
- ☐ .............................

Adventures to Have :

- ☐ .............................
- ☐ .............................
- ☐ .............................
- ☐ .............................
- ☐ .............................
- ☐ .............................

Things to Observe :

- ☐ .............................
- ☐ .............................
- ☐ .............................
- ☐ .............................
- ☐ .............................
- ☐ .............................
- ☐ .............................

Places to Mingle :

- ☐ .............................
- ☐ .............................
- ☐ .............................
- ☐ .............................
- ☐ .............................
- ☐ .............................
- ☐ .............................

Shops to Visit :

- ☐ .............................
- ☐ .............................
- ☐ .............................
- ☐ .............................
- ☐ .............................

Streets to Check Out :

- ☐ .........................
- ☐ .........................
- ☐ .........................

- ☐ .........................
- ☐ .........................
- ☐ .........................

| Date | Itinerary | Reservation |
|---|---|---|
|  |  |  |
|  |  |  |
|  |  |  |
|  |  |  |
|  |  |  |
|  |  |  |
|  |  |  |
|  |  |  |
|  |  |  |
|  |  |  |
|  |  |  |
|  |  |  |
|  |  |  |

## Notes

# Journal

# Travel Adventure Starts Here!

## pre-travel checklist

## packing checklist

venue
travel date/time

travel buddy
transportation

hotel reservation
contact person/number

travel cost
travel budget

Things to See & Do :

☐ .................................
☐ .................................
☐ .................................
☐ .................................
☐ .................................

☐ .................................
☐ .................................
☐ .................................
☐ .................................
☐ .................................

Adventures to Have :

☐ .........................
☐ .........................
☐ .........................
☐ .........................
☐ .........................
☐ .........................
☐ .........................

Things to Observe :

☐ .................................
☐ .................................
☐ .................................
☐ .................................
☐ .................................
☐ .................................
☐ .................................
☐ .................................

Places to Mingle :

☐ .........................
☐ .........................
☐ .........................
☐ .........................
☐ .........................
☐ .........................
☐ .........................

Shops to Visit :

☐ .....................
☐ .....................
☐ .....................
☐ .....................
☐ .....................
☐ .....................

Streets to Check Out :

☐ ......................
☐ ......................
☐ ......................

☐ ......................
☐ ......................
☐ ......................

| Date | Itinerary | Reservation |
|------|-----------|-------------|
|      |           |             |
|      |           |             |
|      |           |             |
|      |           |             |
|      |           |             |
|      |           |             |
|      |           |             |
|      |           |             |
|      |           |             |
|      |           |             |
|      |           |             |
|      |           |             |
|      |           |             |

## Notes

# Journal

# Travel Adventure Starts Here!

## pre-travel checklist

## packing checklist

Contacts

---

venue
travel date/time

_____

travel buddy
transportation

_____

hotel reservation
contact person/number

_____

travel cost
travel budget

_____

Things to See & Do :

☐ ............................
☐ ............................
☐ ............................
☐ ............................
☐ ............................

☐ ............................
☐ ............................
☐ ............................
☐ ............................
☐ ............................

Adventures to Have :

☐ ............................
☐ ............................
☐ ............................
☐ ............................
☐ ............................
☐ ............................
☐ ............................

Things to Observe :

☐ ............................
☐ ............................
☐ ............................
☐ ............................
☐ ............................
☐ ............................
☐ ............................
☐ ............................

Places to Mingle :

☐ ............................
☐ ............................
☐ ............................
☐ ............................
☐ ............................
☐ ............................
☐ ............................

Shops to Visit :

☐ ............................
☐ ............................
☐ ............................
☐ ............................
☐ ............................

Streets to Check Out :

☐ ....................
☐ ....................
☐ ....................

☐ ....................
☐ ....................
☐ ....................

| Date | Itinerary | Reservation |
|------|-----------|-------------|
|      |           |             |
|      |           |             |
|      |           |             |
|      |           |             |
|      |           |             |
|      |           |             |
|      |           |             |
|      |           |             |
|      |           |             |
|      |           |             |
|      |           |             |
|      |           |             |
|      |           |             |

## Notes

# Travel Adventure Starts Here!

## pre-travel checklist

## packing checklist

Contacts

venue
travel date/time

_____

travel buddy
transportation

_____

hotel reservation
contact person/number

_____

travel cost
travel budget

_____

## Things to See & Do :

☐ ...................................
☐ ...................................
☐ ...................................
☐ ...................................
☐ ...................................

☐ ...................................
☐ ...................................
☐ ...................................
☐ ...................................
☐ ...................................

### Adventures to Have :

☐ ...............................
☐ ...............................
☐ ...............................
☐ ...............................
☐ ...............................
☐ ...............................
☐ ...............................

### Things to Observe :

☐ ...............................
☐ ...............................
☐ ...............................
☐ ...............................
☐ ...............................
☐ ...............................
☐ ...............................

### Places to Mingle :

☐ ...............................
☐ ...............................
☐ ...............................
☐ ...............................
☐ ...............................
☐ ...............................
☐ ...............................

### Shops to Visit :

☐ ...............................
☐ ...............................
☐ ...............................
☐ ...............................
☐ ...............................
☐ ...............................

### Streets to Check Out :

☐ ...........................
☐ ...........................
☐ ...........................

☐ ...........................
☐ ...........................
☐ ...........................

| Date | Itinerary | Reservation |
|---|---|---|
| | | |
| | | |
| | | |
| | | |
| | | |
| | | |
| | | |
| | | |
| | | |
| | | |
| | | |
| | | |
| | | |

## Notes

# Journal

# Travel Adventure Starts Here!

## pre-travel checklist

## packing checklist

Contacts

venue
travel date/time

_____

travel buddy
transportation

_____

hotel reservation
contact person/number

_____

travel cost
travel budget

_____

Things to See & Do :

- ☐ ...............................
- ☐ ...............................
- ☐ ...............................
- ☐ ...............................
- ☐ ...............................

- ☐ ...............................
- ☐ ...............................
- ☐ ...............................
- ☐ ...............................
- ☐ ...............................

Adventures to Have :

- ☐ .......................
- ☐ .......................
- ☐ .......................
- ☐ .......................
- ☐ .......................
- ☐ .......................
- ☐ .......................

Things to Observe :

- ☐ ...............................
- ☐ ...............................
- ☐ ...............................
- ☐ ...............................
- ☐ ...............................
- ☐ ...............................

Places to Mingle :

- ☐ .......................
- ☐ .......................
- ☐ .......................
- ☐ .......................
- ☐ .......................
- ☐ .......................
- ☐ .......................

Shops to Visit :

- ☐ .................
- ☐ .................
- ☐ .................
- ☐ .................
- ☐ .................
- ☐ .................

Streets to Check Out :

- ☐ ....................
- ☐ ....................
- ☐ ....................

- ☐ ....................
- ☐ ....................
- ☐ ....................

| Date | Itinerary | Reservation |
|---|---|---|
| | | |
| | | |
| | | |
| | | |
| | | |
| | | |
| | | |
| | | |
| | | |
| | | |
| | | |
| | | |
| | | |

**Notes**

# Journal

# Travel Adventure Starts Here!

## pre-travel checklist

## packing checklist

venue
travel date/time

travel buddy
transportation

hotel reservation
contact person/number

travel cost
travel budget

Things to See & Do :

- ☐ .......................................
- ☐ .......................................
- ☐ .......................................
- ☐ .......................................
- ☐ .......................................

- ☐ .......................................
- ☐ .......................................
- ☐ .......................................
- ☐ .......................................
- ☐ .......................................

Adventures to Have :

- ☐ .............................
- ☐ .............................
- ☐ .............................
- ☐ .............................
- ☐ .............................
- ☐ .............................
- ☐ .............................

Things to Observe :

- ☐ .......................................
- ☐ .......................................
- ☐ .......................................
- ☐ .......................................
- ☐ .......................................
- ☐ .......................................
- ☐ .......................................
- ☐ .......................................

Places to Mingle :

- ☐ .............................
- ☐ .............................
- ☐ .............................
- ☐ .............................
- ☐ .............................
- ☐ .............................
- ☐ .............................

Shops to Visit :

- ☐ .......................
- ☐ .......................
- ☐ .......................
- ☐ .......................
- ☐ .......................
- ☐ .......................

Streets to Check Out :

- ☐ ..........................
- ☐ ..........................
- ☐ ..........................

- ☐ ..........................
- ☐ ..........................
- ☐ ..........................

| Date | Itinerary | Reservation |
|------|-----------|-------------|
|      |           |             |
|      |           |             |
|      |           |             |
|      |           |             |
|      |           |             |
|      |           |             |
|      |           |             |
|      |           |             |
|      |           |             |
|      |           |             |
|      |           |             |
|      |           |             |
|      |           |             |

## Notes

# Journal

# Travel Adventure Starts Here!

## pre-travel checklist

## packing checklist

Contacts

---

venue
travel date/time

_____

travel buddy
transportation

_____

hotel reservation
contact person/number

_____

travel cost
travel budget

_____

Things to See & Do :

☐ . . . . . . . . . . . . . . . . . . . . . . . . . . .   ☐ . . . . . . . . . . . . . . . . . . . . . . . . . . .
☐ . . . . . . . . . . . . . . . . . . . . . . . . . . .   ☐ . . . . . . . . . . . . . . . . . . . . . . . . . . .
☐ . . . . . . . . . . . . . . . . . . . . . . . . . . .   ☐ . . . . . . . . . . . . . . . . . . . . . . . . . . .
☐ . . . . . . . . . . . . . . . . . . . . . . . . . . .   ☐ . . . . . . . . . . . . . . . . . . . . . . . . . . .
☐ . . . . . . . . . . . . . . . . . . . . . . . . . . .   ☐ . . . . . . . . . . . . . . . . . . . . . . . . . . .

Adventures to Have :

☐ . . . . . . . . . . . . . . . . . . . . . .
☐ . . . . . . . . . . . . . . . . . . . . . .
☐ . . . . . . . . . . . . . . . . . . . . . .
☐ . . . . . . . . . . . . . . . . . . . . . .
☐ . . . . . . . . . . . . . . . . . . . . . .
☐ . . . . . . . . . . . . . . . . . . . . . .
☐ . . . . . . . . . . . . . . . . . . . . . .

Things to Observe :

☐ . . . . . . . . . . . . . . . . . . . . . . . . . . .
☐ . . . . . . . . . . . . . . . . . . . . . . . . . . .
☐ . . . . . . . . . . . . . . . . . . . . . . . . . . .
☐ . . . . . . . . . . . . . . . . . . . . . . . . . . .
☐ . . . . . . . . . . . . . . . . . . . . . . . . . . .
☐ . . . . . . . . . . . . . . . . . . . . . . . . . . .
☐ . . . . . . . . . . . . . . . . . . . . . . . . . . .

Places to Mingle :

☐ . . . . . . . . . . . . . . . . . . . . . .
☐ . . . . . . . . . . . . . . . . . . . . . .
☐ . . . . . . . . . . . . . . . . . . . . . .
☐ . . . . . . . . . . . . . . . . . . . . . .
☐ . . . . . . . . . . . . . . . . . . . . . .
☐ . . . . . . . . . . . . . . . . . . . . . .
☐ . . . . . . . . . . . . . . . . . . . . . .

Shops to Visit :

☐ . . . . . . . . . . . . . . . . . . . . . .
☐ . . . . . . . . . . . . . . . . . . . . . .
☐ . . . . . . . . . . . . . . . . . . . . . .
☐ . . . . . . . . . . . . . . . . . . . . . .
☐ . . . . . . . . . . . . . . . . . . . . . .
☐ . . . . . . . . . . . . . . . . . . . . . .

Streets to Check Out :

☐ . . . . . . . . . . . . . . . . . . . . .   ☐ . . . . . . . . . . . . . . . . . . . .
☐ . . . . . . . . . . . . . . . . . . . . .   ☐ . . . . . . . . . . . . . . . . . . . .
☐ . . . . . . . . . . . . . . . . . . . . .   ☐ . . . . . . . . . . . . . . . . . . . .

| Date | Itinerary | Reservation |
|---|---|---|
|  |  |  |
|  |  |  |
|  |  |  |
|  |  |  |
|  |  |  |
|  |  |  |
|  |  |  |
|  |  |  |
|  |  |  |
|  |  |  |
|  |  |  |
|  |  |  |
|  |  |  |

## Notes

Journal

# Travel Adventure Starts Here!

## pre-travel checklist

## packing checklist

venue
travel date/time

travel buddy
transportation

hotel reservation
contact person/number

travel cost
travel budget

Things to See & Do :

☐ ...................................
☐ ...................................
☐ ...................................
☐ ...................................
☐ ...................................

☐ ...................................
☐ ...................................
☐ ...................................
☐ ...................................
☐ ...................................

Adventures to Have :

☐ ...........................
☐ ...........................
☐ ...........................
☐ ...........................
☐ ...........................
☐ ...........................
☐ ...........................

Things to Observe :

☐ ...................................
☐ ...................................
☐ ...................................
☐ ...................................
☐ ...................................
☐ ...................................
☐ ...................................

Places to Mingle :

☐ ...........................
☐ ...........................
☐ ...........................
☐ ...........................
☐ ...........................
☐ ...........................
☐ ...........................

Shops to Visit :

☐ ...........................
☐ ...........................
☐ ...........................
☐ ...........................
☐ ...........................
☐ ...........................
☐ ...........................

Streets to Check Out :

☐ .........................
☐ .........................
☐ .........................

☐ .........................
☐ .........................
☐ .........................

| Date | Itinerary | Reservation |
|------|-----------|-------------|
|      |           |             |
|      |           |             |
|      |           |             |
|      |           |             |
|      |           |             |
|      |           |             |
|      |           |             |
|      |           |             |
|      |           |             |
|      |           |             |
|      |           |             |
|      |           |             |
|      |           |             |
|      |           |             |

## Notes

# Journal

# Travel Adventure Starts Here!

## pre-travel checklist

## packing checklist

venue
travel date/time

travel buddy
transportation

hotel reservation
contact person/number

travel cost
travel budget

Things to See & Do :

❑ . . . . . . . . . . . . . . . . . . . . . . . . . . .   ❑ . . . . . . . . . . . . . . . . . . . . . . . . . . .
❑ . . . . . . . . . . . . . . . . . . . . . . . . . . .   ❑ . . . . . . . . . . . . . . . . . . . . . . . . . . .
❑ . . . . . . . . . . . . . . . . . . . . . . . . . . .   ❑ . . . . . . . . . . . . . . . . . . . . . . . . . . .
❑ . . . . . . . . . . . . . . . . . . . . . . . . . . .   ❑ . . . . . . . . . . . . . . . . . . . . . . . . . . .
❑ . . . . . . . . . . . . . . . . . . . . . . . . . . .   ❑ . . . . . . . . . . . . . . . . . . . . . . . . . . .

Adventures to Have :

❑ . . . . . . . . . . . . . . . . . . . .
❑ . . . . . . . . . . . . . . . . . . . .
❑ . . . . . . . . . . . . . . . . . . . .
❑ . . . . . . . . . . . . . . . . . . . .
❑ . . . . . . . . . . . . . . . . . . . .
❑ . . . . . . . . . . . . . . . . . . . .
❑ . . . . . . . . . . . . . . . . . . . .

Things to Observe :

❑ . . . . . . . . . . . . . . . . . . . . . . . . . .
❑ . . . . . . . . . . . . . . . . . . . . . . . . . .
❑ . . . . . . . . . . . . . . . . . . . . . . . . . .
❑ . . . . . . . . . . . . . . . . . . . . . . . . . .
❑ . . . . . . . . . . . . . . . . . . . . . . . . . .
❑ . . . . . . . . . . . . . . . . . . . . . . . . . .
❑ . . . . . . . . . . . . . . . . . . . . . . . . . .

Places to Mingle :

❑ . . . . . . . . . . . . . . . . . . . .
❑ . . . . . . . . . . . . . . . . . . . .
❑ . . . . . . . . . . . . . . . . . . . .
❑ . . . . . . . . . . . . . . . . . . . .
❑ . . . . . . . . . . . . . . . . . . . .
❑ . . . . . . . . . . . . . . . . . . . .
❑ . . . . . . . . . . . . . . . . . . . .

Shops to Visit :

❑ . . . . . . . . . . . . . . . . . . . .
❑ . . . . . . . . . . . . . . . . . . . .
❑ . . . . . . . . . . . . . . . . . . . .
❑ . . . . . . . . . . . . . . . . . . . .
❑ . . . . . . . . . . . . . . . . . . . .
❑ . . . . . . . . . . . . . . . . . . . .
❑ . . . . . . . . . . . . . . . . . . . .

Streets to Check Out :

❑ . . . . . . . . . . . . . . . . . . . . . .   ❑ . . . . . . . . . . . . . . . . . . . .
❑ . . . . . . . . . . . . . . . . . . . . . .   ❑ . . . . . . . . . . . . . . . . . . . .
❑ . . . . . . . . . . . . . . . . . . . . . .   ❑ . . . . . . . . . . . . . . . . . . . .

| Date | Itinerary | Reservation |
|------|-----------|-------------|
|      |           |             |
|      |           |             |
|      |           |             |
|      |           |             |
|      |           |             |
|      |           |             |
|      |           |             |
|      |           |             |
|      |           |             |
|      |           |             |
|      |           |             |
|      |           |             |
|      |           |             |
|      |           |             |

## Notes

# Journal

# Travel Adventure Starts Here!

## pre-travel checklist

## packing checklist

Contacts

---

venue
travel date/time

_____

travel buddy
transportation

_____

hotel reservation
contact person/number

_____

travel cost
travel budget

_____

## Things to See & Do :

🚩 ..................................

🚩 ..................................

🚩 ..................................

🚩 ..................................

🚩 ..................................

🚩 ..................................

🚩 ..................................

🚩 ..................................

🚩 ..................................

🚩 ..................................

### Adventures to Have :

🚩 ..........................

🚩 ..........................

🚩 ..........................

🚩 ..........................

🚩 ..........................

🚩 ..........................

🚩 ..........................

### Things to Observe :

🚩 ..................................

🚩 ..................................

🚩 ..................................

🚩 ..................................

🚩 ..................................

🚩 ..................................

🚩 ..................................

### Places to Mingle :

🚩 ..........................

🚩 ..........................

🚩 ..........................

🚩 ..........................

🚩 ..........................

🚩 ..........................

🚩 ..........................

### Shops to Visit :

🚩 ....................

🚩 ....................

🚩 ....................

🚩 ....................

🚩 ....................

🚩 ....................

🚩 ....................

### Streets to Check Out :

🚩 ........................

🚩 ........................

🚩 ........................

🚩 ........................

🚩 ........................

🚩 ........................

| Date | Itinerary | Reservation |
|---|---|---|
| | | |
| | | |
| | | |
| | | |
| | | |
| | | |
| | | |
| | | |
| | | |
| | | |
| | | |
| | | |
| | | |

**Notes**

# Journal

# Travel Adventure Starts Here!

## pre-travel checklist

## packing checklist

venue
travel date/time

travel buddy
transportation

hotel reservation
contact person/number

travel cost
travel budget

Things to See & Do :

- ☐ . . . . . . . . . . . . . . . . . . . . . . . . .
- ☐ . . . . . . . . . . . . . . . . . . . . . . . . .
- ☐ . . . . . . . . . . . . . . . . . . . . . . . . .
- ☐ . . . . . . . . . . . . . . . . . . . . . . . . .
- ☐ . . . . . . . . . . . . . . . . . . . . . . . . .

- ☐ . . . . . . . . . . . . . . . . . . . . . . . . .
- ☐ . . . . . . . . . . . . . . . . . . . . . . . . .
- ☐ . . . . . . . . . . . . . . . . . . . . . . . . .
- ☐ . . . . . . . . . . . . . . . . . . . . . . . . .
- ☐ . . . . . . . . . . . . . . . . . . . . . . . . .

Adventures to Have :

- ☐ . . . . . . . . . . . . . . . . . . . .
- ☐ . . . . . . . . . . . . . . . . . . . .
- ☐ . . . . . . . . . . . . . . . . . . . .
- ☐ . . . . . . . . . . . . . . . . . . . .
- ☐ . . . . . . . . . . . . . . . . . . . .
- ☐ . . . . . . . . . . . . . . . . . . . .

Things to Observe :

- ☐ . . . . . . . . . . . . . . . . . . . . . . . . .
- ☐ . . . . . . . . . . . . . . . . . . . . . . . . .
- ☐ . . . . . . . . . . . . . . . . . . . . . . . . .
- ☐ . . . . . . . . . . . . . . . . . . . . . . . . .
- ☐ . . . . . . . . . . . . . . . . . . . . . . . . .
- ☐ . . . . . . . . . . . . . . . . . . . . . . . . .
- ☐ . . . . . . . . . . . . . . . . . . . . . . . . .

Places to Mingle :

- ☐ . . . . . . . . . . . . . . . . . . . .
- ☐ . . . . . . . . . . . . . . . . . . . .
- ☐ . . . . . . . . . . . . . . . . . . . .
- ☐ . . . . . . . . . . . . . . . . . . . .
- ☐ . . . . . . . . . . . . . . . . . . . .
- ☐ . . . . . . . . . . . . . . . . . . . .
- ☐ . . . . . . . . . . . . . . . . . . . .

Shops to Visit :

- ☐ . . . . . . . . . . . . . . . . . . .
- ☐ . . . . . . . . . . . . . . . . . . .
- ☐ . . . . . . . . . . . . . . . . . . .
- ☐ . . . . . . . . . . . . . . . . . . .
- ☐ . . . . . . . . . . . . . . . . . . .
- ☐ . . . . . . . . . . . . . . . . . . .

Streets to Check Out :

- ☐ . . . . . . . . . . . . . . . . . . . .
- ☐ . . . . . . . . . . . . . . . . . . . .
- ☐ . . . . . . . . . . . . . . . . . . . .

- ☐ . . . . . . . . . . . . . . . . . . . .
- ☐ . . . . . . . . . . . . . . . . . . . .
- ☐ . . . . . . . . . . . . . . . . . . . .

| Date | Itinerary | Reservation |
| --- | --- | --- |
| | | |
| | | |
| | | |
| | | |
| | | |
| | | |
| | | |
| | | |
| | | |
| | | |
| | | |
| | | |

## Notes

# Journal

# Travel Adventure Starts Here!

## pre-travel checklist

## packing checklist

Contacts

venue
travel date/time

_____

travel buddy
transportation

_____

hotel reservation
contact person/number

_____

travel cost
travel budget

_____

Things to See & Do :

☐ . . . . . . . . . . . . . . . . . . . . . .    ☐ . . . . . . . . . . . . . . . . . . . . . .
☐ . . . . . . . . . . . . . . . . . . . . . .    ☐ . . . . . . . . . . . . . . . . . . . . . .
☐ . . . . . . . . . . . . . . . . . . . . . .    ☐ . . . . . . . . . . . . . . . . . . . . . .
☐ . . . . . . . . . . . . . . . . . . . . . .    ☐ . . . . . . . . . . . . . . . . . . . . . .
☐ . . . . . . . . . . . . . . . . . . . . . .    ☐ . . . . . . . . . . . . . . . . . . . . . .

Adventures to Have :

☐ . . . . . . . . . . . . . . . .
☐ . . . . . . . . . . . . . . . .
☐ . . . . . . . . . . . . . . . .
☐ . . . . . . . . . . . . . . . .
☐ . . . . . . . . . . . . . . . .
☐ . . . . . . . . . . . . . . . .
☐ . . . . . . . . . . . . . . . .

Things to Observe :

☐ . . . . . . . . . . . . . . . . . . . . . .
☐ . . . . . . . . . . . . . . . . . . . . . .
☐ . . . . . . . . . . . . . . . . . . . . . .
☐ . . . . . . . . . . . . . . . . . . . . . .
☐ . . . . . . . . . . . . . . . . . . . . . .
☐ . . . . . . . . . . . . . . . . . . . . . .
☐ . . . . . . . . . . . . . . . . . . . . . .
☐ . . . . . . . . . . . . . . . . . . . . . .

Places to Mingle :

☐ . . . . . . . . . . . . . . . .
☐ . . . . . . . . . . . . . . . .
☐ . . . . . . . . . . . . . . . .
☐ . . . . . . . . . . . . . . . .
☐ . . . . . . . . . . . . . . . .
☐ . . . . . . . . . . . . . . . .
☐ . . . . . . . . . . . . . . . .

Shops to Visit :

☐ . . . . . . . . . . . . . . . .
☐ . . . . . . . . . . . . . . . .
☐ . . . . . . . . . . . . . . . .
☐ . . . . . . . . . . . . . . . .
☐ . . . . . . . . . . . . . . . .
☐ . . . . . . . . . . . . . . . .
☐ . . . . . . . . . . . . . . . .

Streets to Check Out :

☐ . . . . . . . . . . . . . . . . . .    ☐ . . . . . . . . . . . . . . . . . .
☐ . . . . . . . . . . . . . . . . . .    ☐ . . . . . . . . . . . . . . . . . .
☐ . . . . . . . . . . . . . . . . . .    ☐ . . . . . . . . . . . . . . . . . .

| Date | Itinerary | Reservation |
|------|-----------|-------------|
|      |           |             |
|      |           |             |
|      |           |             |
|      |           |             |
|      |           |             |
|      |           |             |
|      |           |             |
|      |           |             |
|      |           |             |
|      |           |             |
|      |           |             |
|      |           |             |
|      |           |             |
|      |           |             |

## Notes

# Journal

# Travel Adventure Starts Here!

## pre-travel checklist

## packing checklist

venue
travel date/time

travel buddy
transportation

hotel reservation
contact person/number

travel cost
travel budget

Things to See & Do :

☐ . . . . . . . . . . . . . . . . . . . . . . . .     ☐ . . . . . . . . . . . . . . . . . . . . . . . .
☐ . . . . . . . . . . . . . . . . . . . . . . . .     ☐ . . . . . . . . . . . . . . . . . . . . . . . .
☐ . . . . . . . . . . . . . . . . . . . . . . . .     ☐ . . . . . . . . . . . . . . . . . . . . . . . .
☐ . . . . . . . . . . . . . . . . . . . . . . . .     ☐ . . . . . . . . . . . . . . . . . . . . . . . .
☐ . . . . . . . . . . . . . . . . . . . . . . . .     ☐ . . . . . . . . . . . . . . . . . . . . . . . .

Adventures to Have :

☐ . . . . . . . . . . . . . . . . . . . .
☐ . . . . . . . . . . . . . . . . . . . .
☐ . . . . . . . . . . . . . . . . . . . .
☐ . . . . . . . . . . . . . . . . . . . .
☐ . . . . . . . . . . . . . . . . . . . .
☐ . . . . . . . . . . . . . . . . . . . .
☐ . . . . . . . . . . . . . . . . . . . .

Things to Observe :

☐ . . . . . . . . . . . . . . . . . . . . . . . .
☐ . . . . . . . . . . . . . . . . . . . . . . . .
☐ . . . . . . . . . . . . . . . . . . . . . . . .
☐ . . . . . . . . . . . . . . . . . . . . . . . .
☐ . . . . . . . . . . . . . . . . . . . . . . . .
☐ . . . . . . . . . . . . . . . . . . . . . . . .
☐ . . . . . . . . . . . . . . . . . . . . . . . .

Places to Mingle :

☐ . . . . . . . . . . . . . . . . . . . .
☐ . . . . . . . . . . . . . . . . . . . .
☐ . . . . . . . . . . . . . . . . . . . .
☐ . . . . . . . . . . . . . . . . . . . .
☐ . . . . . . . . . . . . . . . . . . . .
☐ . . . . . . . . . . . . . . . . . . . .
☐ . . . . . . . . . . . . . . . . . . . .

Shops to Visit :

☐ . . . . . . . . . . . . . . . . . . . .
☐ . . . . . . . . . . . . . . . . . . . .
☐ . . . . . . . . . . . . . . . . . . . .
☐ . . . . . . . . . . . . . . . . . . . .
☐ . . . . . . . . . . . . . . . . . . . .
☐ . . . . . . . . . . . . . . . . . . . .

Streets to Check Out :

☐ . . . . . . . . . . . . . . . . . .     ☐ . . . . . . . . . . . . . . . . . .
☐ . . . . . . . . . . . . . . . . . .     ☐ . . . . . . . . . . . . . . . . . .
☐ . . . . . . . . . . . . . . . . . .     ☐ . . . . . . . . . . . . . . . . . .

| Date | Itinerary | Reservation |
|------|-----------|-------------|
|      |           |             |
|      |           |             |
|      |           |             |
|      |           |             |
|      |           |             |
|      |           |             |
|      |           |             |
|      |           |             |
|      |           |             |
|      |           |             |
|      |           |             |
|      |           |             |
|      |           |             |
|      |           |             |
|      |           |             |

## Notes

# Journal

# Travel Adventure Starts Here!

## pre-travel checklist

## packing checklist

Contacts

---

venue
travel date/time

travel buddy
transportation

hotel reservation
contact person/number

travel cost
travel budget

Things to See & Do :

❑ ........................................
❑ ........................................
❑ ........................................
❑ ........................................
❑ ........................................

❑ ........................................
❑ ........................................
❑ ........................................
❑ ........................................
❑ ........................................

Adventures to Have :

❑ .............................
❑ .............................
❑ .............................
❑ .............................
❑ .............................
❑ .............................
❑ .............................

Things to Observe :

❑ ........................................
❑ ........................................
❑ ........................................
❑ ........................................
❑ ........................................
❑ ........................................
❑ ........................................

Places to Mingle :

❑ .............................
❑ .............................
❑ .............................
❑ .............................
❑ .............................
❑ .............................
❑ .............................

Shops to Visit :

❑ ........................
❑ ........................
❑ ........................
❑ ........................
❑ ........................
❑ ........................
❑ ........................

Streets to Check Out :

❑ ........................
❑ ........................
❑ ........................

❑ ........................
❑ ........................
❑ ........................

| Date | Itinerary | Reservation |
|------|-----------|-------------|
|      |           |             |
|      |           |             |
|      |           |             |
|      |           |             |
|      |           |             |
|      |           |             |
|      |           |             |
|      |           |             |
|      |           |             |
|      |           |             |
|      |           |             |
|      |           |             |

## Notes

# Journal

# Travel Adventure Starts Here!

## pre-travel checklist

## packing checklist

venue
travel date/time

travel buddy
transportation

hotel reservation
contact person/number

travel cost
travel budget

Things to See & Do :

☐ ..................................... ☐ .....................................
☐ ..................................... ☐ .....................................
☐ ..................................... ☐ .....................................
☐ ..................................... ☐ .....................................
☐ ..................................... ☐ .....................................

Adventures to Have :

☐ .............................
☐ .............................
☐ .............................
☐ .............................
☐ .............................
☐ .............................
☐ .............................

Things to Observe :

☐ .....................................
☐ .....................................
☐ .....................................
☐ .....................................
☐ .....................................
☐ .....................................
☐ .....................................
☐ .....................................

Places to Mingle :

☐ .............................
☐ .............................
☐ .............................
☐ .............................
☐ .............................
☐ .............................
☐ .............................

Shops to Visit :

☐ .........................
☐ .........................
☐ .........................
☐ .........................
☐ .........................
☐ .........................
☐ .........................

Streets to Check Out :

☐ ........................... ☐ ...........................
☐ ........................... ☐ ...........................
☐ ........................... ☐ ...........................

| Date | Itinerary | Reservation |
|------|-----------|-------------|
|      |           |             |
|      |           |             |
|      |           |             |
|      |           |             |
|      |           |             |
|      |           |             |
|      |           |             |
|      |           |             |
|      |           |             |
|      |           |             |
|      |           |             |
|      |           |             |
|      |           |             |

## Notes

# Journal

# Travel Adventure Starts Here!

## pre-travel checklist

## packing checklist

Contacts

---

venue
travel date/time

_____

travel buddy
transportation

_____

hotel reservation
contact person/number

_____

travel cost
travel budget

_____

Things to See & Do :

☐ ............................
☐ ............................
☐ ............................
☐ ............................
☐ ............................

☐ ............................
☐ ............................
☐ ............................
☐ ............................
☐ ............................

Adventures to Have :

☐ ....................
☐ ....................
☐ ....................
☐ ....................
☐ ....................
☐ ....................
☐ ....................

Things to Observe :

☐ ............................
☐ ............................
☐ ............................
☐ ............................
☐ ............................
☐ ............................
☐ ............................

Places to Mingle :

☐ ....................
☐ ....................
☐ ....................
☐ ....................
☐ ....................
☐ ....................
☐ ....................

Shops to Visit :

☐ ....................
☐ ....................
☐ ....................
☐ ....................
☐ ....................
☐ ....................

Streets to Check Out :

☐ ....................
☐ ....................
☐ ....................

☐ ....................
☐ ....................
☐ ....................

| Date | Itinerary | Reservation |
|------|-----------|-------------|
|      |           |             |
|      |           |             |
|      |           |             |
|      |           |             |
|      |           |             |
|      |           |             |
|      |           |             |
|      |           |             |
|      |           |             |
|      |           |             |
|      |           |             |
|      |           |             |
|      |           |             |

## Notes

# Journal

# Travel Adventure Starts Here!

## pre-travel checklist

## packing checklist

---

**venue**
**travel date/time**

**travel buddy**
**transportation**

**hotel reservation**
**contact person/number**

**travel cost**
**travel budget**

Things to See & Do :

☐ ....................  ☐ ....................
☐ ....................  ☐ ....................
☐ ....................  ☐ ....................
☐ ....................  ☐ ....................
☐ ....................  ☐ ....................

Adventures to Have :

☐ ..................
☐ ..................
☐ ..................
☐ ..................
☐ ..................
☐ ..................
☐ ..................

Things to Observe :

☐ ....................
☐ ....................
☐ ....................
☐ ....................
☐ ....................
☐ ....................
☐ ....................
☐ ....................

Places to Mingle :

☐ ..................
☐ ..................
☐ ..................
☐ ..................
☐ ..................
☐ ..................
☐ ..................

Shops to Visit :

☐ ..................
☐ ..................
☐ ..................
☐ ..................
☐ ..................
☐ ..................
☐ ..................

Streets to Check Out :

☐ ..................  ☐ ..................
☐ ..................  ☐ ..................
☐ ..................  ☐ ..................

| Date | Itinerary | Reservation |
|------|-----------|-------------|
|      |           |             |
|      |           |             |
|      |           |             |
|      |           |             |
|      |           |             |
|      |           |             |
|      |           |             |
|      |           |             |
|      |           |             |
|      |           |             |
|      |           |             |
|      |           |             |
|      |           |             |

## Notes

# Journal

www.ingramcontent.com/pod-product-compliance
Lightning Source LLC
Chambersburg PA
CBHW081337090426
42737CB00017B/3178